MW01283512

213
Silly
Drawing
Prompts
for Kids

Copyright © 2017 New Life Overnight

All rights reserved.

ISBN-13: 978-1545300718
ISBN-10: 1545300712

DRAW a cartoon strawberry eating a hot dog

Example drawing

Every page gives you an idea of something silly to draw. Use your imagination. There is no right or wrong way to do it. Feel free to add your own creative touch to each drawing. Just have fun!

CAUTION! Some ideas may be too silly for adults.

DRAW a bald man with long ears

DRAW a flea circus

DRAW a penguin riding a skateboard

DRAW a dinosaur riding on a tricycle

DRAW a pirate riding a huge yellow rubber ducky

DRAW a baby monkey wearing a diaper and carrying a lollipop

DRAW a whale wearing a suit and tie

DRAW horses playing horseshoes

DRAW a pretzel doing gymnastics

DRAW a fish wearing roller skates

DRAW a girl with very short legs and very long arms

DRAW an overweight banana exercising at the gym

DRAW a giant carrot chasing a rabbit

DRAW a tall toad playing basketball

DRAW a fire breathing kitten

DRAW a bear wearing a tutu and playing the tuba

DRAW a llama wearing pajamas

DRAW a cow in a bathtub full of cotton candy

DRAW a cartoon doughnut with a cowboy hat riding a lobster

DRAW a grandma grasshopper knitting a sweater

DRAW a mouse with a dinosaur tail playing a harp

DRAW a piece of pizza directing traffic

DRAW a shark skydiving from an airplane

DRAW a bar of soap taking a mud bath

DRAW a polka dot book reading a newspaper

DRAW a cartoon candy bar blowing a giant bubble gum bubble

DRAW a flamingo swimming in a fish bowl

DRAW a dolphin with wings flying upside down

DRAW a giant spider driving a tiny car

DRAW a roach wearing long socks while playing piano on the moon

DRAW a pigeon in a space ship flying through the dessert

DRAW an ant eater riding a jet ski in a bowl of soup

DRAW a hairy butterfly playing golf in outer space

DRAW a duck in a dress sitting at a bus stop

DRAW a smelly hippo on stilts climbing a volcano

DRAW a zebra in a bunny suit walking a tight rope

DRAW a skinny giraffe with a jetpack

DRAW a frog with bunny ears and large glasses

DRAW a fly with huge muscles eating spaghetti

DRAW an acorn wearing a top hat while snorkeling

DRAW an octopus wearing rubber boots fishing for hamburgers

DRAW a cartoon pumpkin playing baseball

DRAW a puppy mowing grass on a rainy day

DRAW a mouse riding a hoverboard

DRAW a hamster playing drums made out of old car parts

DRAW a swordfish climbing a mountain made of jelly

DRAW a fish playing peekaboo

DRAW a crime fighting princess

DRAW a banana with legs like a caterpillar

DRAW a car that is shaped like an onion

DRAW a sea shell with bad breath

DRAW a ten-story sand castle with crab soldiers guarding it

DRAW a piece of celery playing the guitar

DRAW a doughnut looking in a fun house mirror

DRAW a sheep doing a high dive off of a waterfall

DRAW a bag of chips climbing a tree

DRAW a candy bar dressed up like a country music singer

DRAW a piece of broccoli shopping for groceries

DRAW a cartoon square and a cartoon circle holding hands and walking into the sunset

DRAW an open book where the drawings are coming to life

DRAW a cartoon marker hopping on a pogo stick

DRAW a grandmother riding a skateboard

DRAW an alligator dressed up as a doctor

DRAW a cartoon dog eating a banana split sundae

DRAW a cartoon fork and spoon eating dinner together

DRAW a cartoon towel swimming in a pool

DRAW a house made out of clouds

DRAW a cartoon sun with glasses drinking iced tea

DRAW a grandfather with a plaid parachute

DRAW an airplane with wings like a bird

DRAW a baby pushing her mother in a stroller

DRAW a tap dancing lizard wearing a jester's hat

DRAW a peacock doing karate

DRAW an elephant with very long toe nails

DRAW a panda bear wearing a space suit

DRAW a hamburger running on a tread mill

DRAW an owl using binoculars

DRAW a muscle building beaver carrying a giant log

DRAW a bowl of colorful socks

DRAW a scuba diver swimming in a pile of leaves

DRAW a squid flying a fighter jet

DRAW a castle made out of cheese

DRAW a birthday cake with grass growing on top

DRAW a small foot in a large shoe

DRAW a piece of cheese running from a cheese grater

DRAW an apple with a bow and arrow

DRAW a cricket dressed up like a cowboy

DRAW an ant playing the saxophone

DRAW a picture of yourself drawing a picture

DRAW a pair of false teeth chasing an ice-cream cone

DRAW a cartoon lightbulb dressed as a crime fighting superhero

DRAW a mansion made out of candy, cake, and ice-cream

DRAW a lava monster dressed up like a baby

DRAW a bowl of alphabet soup

DRAW a gorilla riding on an ostrich

DRAW nacho chips swimming in a pool of cheese dip

DRAW cartoon peas dressed as medieval soldiers

DRAW a lizard riding a jet powered bicycle

DRAW a penguin surfing on an alligator

DRAW a hairy pickle with polka dots

DRAW a cartoon telephone typing on the computer

DRAW a dinosaur with a head like a kitten

DRAW a construction worker flying a kite

DRAW gummy bears bouncing on a trampoline

DRAW a baby crocodile in a diaper throwing a temper tantrum

DRAW a giant hamster attacking a city

DRAW a horse with a backpack on his first day of school

DRAW a house shaped like a cowboy hat

DRAW a chipmunk skiing in the desert

DRAW a swordfish fighting a pirate

DRAW a flying cartoon tooth wearing a cape

DRAW a cartoon television reading a book

DRAW a surfing giraffe wearing a tuxedo

DRAW a rhinoceros riding on a four-wheeler ATV

DRAW a pig jumping through a ring of fire on a motorcycle

DRAW a hang gliding taco

DRAW a cartoon fan signing autographs

DRAW a lumberjack chopping down giant broccoli trees

DRAW a potato dressed up as a sumo wrestler

DRAW a tap dancing skunk

DRAW an ice-cream cone sliding down a rainbow

DRAW a burnt piece of toast jumping off a diving board

DRAW a cartoon basketball playing baseball

DRAW a girl holding an umbrella while it is raining candy

DRAW a hummingbird using a jumping rope

DRAW a cartoon carrot wearing flip flops and a large sombrero

DRAW a squirrel juggling acorns

DRAW a pineapple cooking on a bar-b-que grill

DRAW a baby chick wearing its egg shell like an outfit

DRAW a worm driving a military tank

DRAW a worm wrapping itself around a candy cane

DRAW a flag twirling moose wearing sneakers

DRAW a beaver brushing his teeth with a giant toothbrush

DRAW a marching band with invisible instruments

DRAW an army soldier dressed up like a clown

DRAW a mole playing golf

DRAW a giant mushroom castle where ants live

DRAW a cartoon cookie peeking out of his cookie jar

DRAW a plate of eggs and bacon

DRAW an old boot with flowers growing out of it

DRAW a fish dressed like a cowboy

DRAW a group of construction workers riding a merry go round

DRAW a sheep eating a pizza with ice-cream on top

DRAW a grizzly bear riding a child's scooter

DRAW a cartoon lemon driving a beat up old car

DRAW a cartoon turkey eating Thanksgiving dinner

DRAW a slice of cake made out of metal and screws

DRAW a mashed potato mountain with children skiing down it

DRAW cartoon salt and pepper shakers in a boxing match

DRAW a bank robber falling into a man hole

DRAW a deer wearing camouflage while hunting

DRAW an egg who fell down while jumping rope

DRAW a piece of fried chicken going on a picnic

DRAW a penguin frozen in a block of ice

DRAW children swimming in a bucket of popcorn

DRAW a rabbit riding a unicycle on a balance beam

DRAW a turtle who had a pie thrown at his face

DRAW a lion singing opera music

DRAW soldiers squirting each other with water guns

DRAW a cartoon paint bucket painting a polka dot fence

DRAW a monkey teaching a class of students

DRAW a zebra with rainbow stripes

DRAW a ladybug wearing a raincoat

DRAW a cat and a dog playing checkers

DRAW a hippo diving into a kiddie pool

DRAW a bird with carrot shaped wings

DRAW a train with pizza wheels and garlic bread train cars

DRAW a starfish blowing bubbles

DRAW a cartoon chicken nugget eating a French fry

DRAW a talking candy machine with arms and legs

DRAW a jellyfish riding a tricycle

DRAW a slimy snail using a jump rope

DRAW a skyscraper made from popsicle sticks

DRAW a flashlight that shoots fire works

DRAW a cow floating up with a big bunch of balloons in his hand

DRAW an eagle being shot out of a confetti cannon

DRAW a stick figure with a long beard looking at his reflection in the mirror

DRAW a walrus walking on his hands with a hat on his feet

DRAW a pickle shaped space ship

DRAW a rollercoaster made out of liquorish, peppermints, and lollipops

DRAW a person covered entirely with puppies

DRAW a piece of bread taking a nap

DRAW an airplane made out of old shoes

DRAW a caterpillar wearing different kinds of shoes on each foot

DRAW the world's biggest sandwich made out of sand

DRAW a miniature elephant running in a hamster wheel

DRAW an acrobatic sea turtle

DRAW a cartoon pinecone wearing jeans drinking a coffee

DRAW a goat waiter serving food from the dumpster

DRAW a sunburnt polar bear fishing in a boat

DRAW a seahorse in a barn

DRAW a marshmallow walking on the sun

DRAW the world's fastest flying mosquito

DRAW an action figure chopping a tree with his hand

DRAW a porcupine who needs a haircut

DRAW a peanut ironing clothes

DRAW a gym bag full of macaroni and cheese

DRAW a treasure map written on bag of cat food

DRAW a palm tree wearing a hula skirt

DRAW a ferret playing hopscotch

DRAW an upside-down waterfall

Made in the USA
Middletown, DE
16 December 2019

81000945R00124